BEYOND THE
BOTTOM LINE

Beyond the Bottom Line

How Mindful Leadership and Positive Work Culture Drive Profitability

Gigi Gupta

Published by Game Changer Publishing

Paperback ISBN: 978-1-966659-09-9

Hardcover ISBN: 978-1-966659-10-5

Digital ISBN: 978-1-966659-11-2

GC GAME CHANGER
PUBLISHING
www.GameChangerPublishing.com

DEDICATION

To Avni & Avyaan
Thank you, for being my inspiration,
my joy, and my constant cheerleaders.

&

To coffee
Without you, this book would
never have been finished.

READ THIS FIRST

Just to say thanks for buying and reading my book, I would like to give you a free bonus gift, a 1-hour consultation & coaching session with me (a $250 value), no strings attached!

Scan the QR Code:

BEYOND THE BOTTOM LINE

HOW MINDFUL LEADERSHIP AND POSITIVE WORK CULTURE DRIVE PROFITABILITY

GIGI GUPTA

CONTENTS

INTRODUCTION

Hi there, future culture-shaping super leader!

Before we dive into the nitty-gritty of organizational culture, let me take you back in time on my own wild journey of leadership and business ownership. It's a story filled with numerous wins, countless face-palm moments, and invaluable lessons, all served with a side of determination and resilience, along with a generous helping of hope and joy—something I always hold onto and wish for you as well.

Flashback to 2015.

I decided to put all my eggs in one basket and kick-start a franchise ownership journey. Not only was I enthusiastic, I had an unshakable faith in my business model. I truly felt like a child who had just laid hands on the most awesome toy in the universe.

But as it turned out, running a business isn't always a walk in the park. And the constant leadership changes, combined with the struggle of keeping a team together, soon made me rethink everything and made my boat rock. In my first year as a business owner, I felt I was a kind and considerate leader for my team, but retaining a good team was tough, and after much introspection, I understood that the issues we were wrestling with weren't just about who we were hiring, who was in the team, and how much we were paying them, which was very surprising. And these were just the tip of the iceberg of a much deeper issue: our organizational culture.

That light bulb moment was a game changer because it altered my perspective of how I ran my business and my company. I realized that our culture was the guiding light, something that steered our ship—sometimes even right into trouble. It was invisible to us all this time. And this realization didn't just ring a bell in my head; it set me on a research mission. I was on a quest to understand what culture is and how it influences every aspect of a business, from the people we work with to the profits we take in. Knowing how much research was out there was nothing short of eye-opening. It revealed how trivial it seemed that we thought everything was in place when there were actually significant gaps. It felt like I had stumbled upon a new pair of glasses that gave me a fresh outlook on the ever-growing world of business.

Fast forward a couple of years later to when I set my intentions to build a strong and positive culture; Great Culture showed up as the highest labor retention award and one of the most profitable centers of about fifty others. So here, for several years, I thought about one day sharing my journey with other aspiring leaders and business owners. I wanted to tell them that it would be a blessing to know that my experience and research helped them succeed in creating a better culture.

Undoubtedly, we can create a better world by developing one company culture at a time. So, I think it's time we embarked on this grand adventure to learn more about the intriguing world of organizational culture and take a deep dive into its significance, how it impacts your business, and how to shape a culture that brings you growth, profit, and work.

Whether you are a leader trying to improve staff retention or increase profits, a startup owner aiming to spread good vibes in your company, or a business coach advising companies on strategy and culture, this book is your roadmap. Through my personal experiences, insight, and wisdom from various industries, this book serves as a comprehensive guide to building an amazing organizational culture. You'll learn about positive communication tactics and tools for boosting employee engagement for day-to-day hurdles that businesses or companies face. As we deep dive into these topics, my hope is that you'll come away with a deeper understanding of how culture can be our organization's trump card.

Like stumbling upon a hidden treasure, it only feels natural that if the culture is good, if everyone is feeling good, it may be just a good vibe thing, but it's much more than that. So, once we take a closer look, being intentional about creating and building that good culture becomes essential. So, your journey starts here with the commitment to building that amazing culture for a greater impact and profit. So, I would say buckle up and get ready for this ride.

> *"No matter where you are in your journey,*
> *that's exactly where you need to be.*
> *The path forward is always ahead."*
> ~Oprah Winfrey

And remember, in the words of Richard Branson, that clients do not come first; employees come first. If you take care of your employees, they will take care of their clients. So, let's go on this journey together to create a workplace culture where everyone feels valued and success is a shared win.

Welcome aboard!

CHAPTER 1
THE IMPORTANCE OF CULTURE

"Corporate culture is the only sustainable competitive advantage
that is completely within the control of the entrepreneur."
~David Cummings, Co-founder of Pardot

This book is based on a true story. I started my franchise journey back in 2015, full of optimism and big plans. I was just, you know, over the clouds, enthusiastic about owning a business and setting all the processes in motion. It was an educational childcare center.

Around that time, I started to work with different teams—the developers, the architects, the project management team—to set up my business. The business was still several months away from opening when I hired my first director (let's call her Jessie), and we hit it off instantly. It felt like we were set for the long haul. Honestly, I even had this idea buzzing in my head about a YouTube channel, *Gigi and Jessie's Lighthouse Journey*, through which we would promote our center with some fun videos. I began working on the finances and local visibility and collaborated with the other teams, including the developers, architects, and city officials, to build a 10,000-square-foot building on a one-acre plot of land. Meanwhile, Jessie worked tirelessly to get all the licensing sorted with the state of Texas. I was over the moon about what lay ahead.

Fast forward to a month into the honeymoon phase, Jessie quit out of the blue. I was heartbroken and shocked, to say the least. I didn't see it coming. I seriously considered myself the best boss someone could ever have. I was under the impression that I was providing her everything she needed to feel good at work and also was consistently setting her up for success. So, her sudden departure came as a shock to me. When Jessie left, we'd already built a team of six staff members who had started to really connect with her. Her resignation left many staff feeling uncertain, a bit lost, and as if it signaled a major flaw in the company.

Six months later, the second director was out, too. Although she wasn't on the same page as some of Jessie's staff picks, I was surprised; I felt I was running the company the best I could. I provided my staff with everything they needed. I cared about them. I provided them with what I thought this educational child care center needed to thrive. However, I struggled to attract and maintain new staff and a high-performing team, which is what led me to further reflect upon what was going on.

That's when it clicked. I needed to take a hard look at my business and figure out how to create a workplace where people didn't just work but wanted to stay. I wanted them to feel as invested in the company's success as I did. That's what I saw was missing. I felt like they only came there to work, which caused them stress, and I wanted to do anything and everything to resolve that to make them feel better, to make them feel good about their place in the business, and provide them with an ideal working environment.

I also thought about how customer service is focused solely on the customer of the business or company and thus fails to consider its staff. Likewise, a CEO or company leader should also be obliged to provide good customer service to their team. The first six months of the company's development provided much room for self-reflection, research, and self-correction.

Fast forward three years down the line, and my center, my franchise, was recognized for maintaining the highest staff retention rates among fifty other franchise locations. This was a significant achievement for the company, and I went on to receive that award for several consecutive years. On top of that, my center was one of the most profitable locations for five years in a row, which is a great perk I'll take any time.

So, how did that happen, and what changes did I make? I figured out that a positive culture and mindful leadership are the two main ingredients of a highly successful business that go hand in hand. I also understood that the primary reason for employee turnover concerns a lot of culture-related data and comes at a high price. When an employee leaves, the cost of hiring a new staff member is almost double the cost of retaining the same employee.

As the above realizations were important to me, I continued my research to further my knowledge. As a leader and a company owner, I believed that anyone would want to work at my company and that the salaries offered to employees were reasonable. But again, my research led me to think otherwise. As mentioned in Daniel H. Pink's book *Drive*, financial incentives actually bring down the intrinsic motivation that is needed to complete complex tasks. I found this more than surprising.

"Money can extinguish intrinsic motivation, diminish performance, crush creativity, encourage unethical behavior, foster short-term thinking, and become addictive."
~Daniel H. Pink

It was not just that I was compensating my staff very well; there was much more to it. The compensation was just the tip of the iceberg, a small part of the company culture that would make my team feel great while working at my company. So, that's what this book is about— what makes a good company culture.

Company culture is defined as a company's personality. It's the sum of what employees think, say, and do while working together and reflects both written and unwritten rules.

When you are looking to change a habit or build a new one, you need to work on it. You need to put in some discipline and be repetitive to put in those changes and actually see the results coming together. It's about building a certain personality for the company that is pleasant and lets you know how people feel on a day-to-day basis. Your team needs to feel so good they just don't want to leave; their heart must be in it. Company culture is a group habit, so even more intention and work are needed.

Culture also includes *unwritten rules* such as, "We only play country music in the front lobby," or "Only Ms. Donna can touch the paper towels; no one else can touch them!" These rules won't be found in the handbook, but they do add to the personality and culture of the company!

The example I consider here is an educational child care center, a high-stress environment. There are a lot of things that keep a staff there, which I'll talk about in the following chapters. For instance:

- What's the purpose or vision they're working toward?
- How do they feel working there on a day-to-day basis?
- How is the leadership?
- What are the values of the company's leaders?
- How do they feel about working for them?
- How would you describe the overall atmosphere at the company?
- Do the employees want to come in every day?
- When they come to work, do they feel good about it?

I found out that it's much deeper than how much employees are paid or what benefits they receive, if any. Financial incentives are important, but culture is what retains the employees for longer and fosters their commitment to building a high-performing team. It is the values and vision of the company that resonate with the employees. I believe that culture is at the heart of it. The topic of how to build an amazing culture often feels endless, but it is, in fact, in a state of constant evolution.

Leaders are the starting point of any organization. Therefore, they need to be alert and adaptive to a constantly changing world. So, what do we, as leaders, provide our staff and teams with so that they feel cared about and evolve into better teams and healthier people in general? It takes leaders and the company as a whole to develop a positive cycle.

" Happy bees make tasty honey."
~Anonymous

The quote above really resonates with me. It's obvious to me that when team members are happy, whatever they are working on—whether it be customer service, coding, or building a product—will impact the company from bottom to top. All this may sound obvious, but believe me, it's not that obvious in the numbers and research, nor is it easy to spot in companies working toward developing their culture. Now, I've noticed more people talking about what makes a good culture, but there's still a long way to go. By that, I mean culture is something you continuously build. You start with a certain team, and as a leader, you train and develop them. Over time, new people join, and the existing staff can mentor the newcomers.

This is how organizations can work toward holding the team together, as well as themselves. Building the company's personality takes a lot of work and collective intention. This is essentially what keeps teams together and prevents employee turnover. And there is a lot more action that can be taken, which I will discuss in the following chapters.

Many staff have also taken on the trend of *"quiet quitting,"* which is a very recent term that refers to doing as little as possible at work but not actually quitting. This is something else that can be addressed with intentional action and several actions toward a better culture. Further, having an anonymous feedback box really helped my business. If a staff member is just not feeling right and they're not able to come up and speak out about an issue that bothers them, they can always provide anonymous feedback. As a whole, it comes down to the leader, who almost always cares about their team, which is very natural.

When the leaders care, the team cares in turn. Likewise, when the leaders listen to their team, the team listens to the leaders.

However, this is not the strategy in place at most companies. Rather, a "command-and-control" leadership style is far more common; you set their responsibilities and give them a list of tasks the staff is supposed to do. Then they get paid, and then they go home. But if you're playing the long game—or as author Simon Sinek calls it, *The Infinite Game*—I love that.

> *"It doesn't even matter whether they are playing*
> *with a finite or an infinite mindset so*
> *long as we are playing with an infinite mindset...*
> *We don't need to admire everything about them,*
> *agree with them, or even like them. We simply*
> *acknowledge that they have strengths and abilities*
> *from which we could learn a thing or two."*
> ~Simon Sinek, *The Infinite Game*

You can implement a transactional leadership style to meet your numbers, but if you want to go above and beyond and if you're considering profits, this is something you really need to take a hard look at. Building the culture from the inside is good for the team, the leaders, the company—everyone.

Here's some Research and data:

- 94% of employees would stay at a company longer if it invested in their careers (Linkedin)
- Companies where employees received regular recognition lead to higher productivity, lower turnover rates, and 21% more profit. (Gallup)
- Employees who feel their voice is heard at work are 4.6 times more likely to perform their best work. (Forbes)
- Companies with strong, positive cultures have been shown to outperform their competitors by up to 202% in terms of financial performance. Revenue growth has been 507% higher over 10 years. This is attributed to higher employee engagement and productivity. (Deloitte)
- Companies with strong cultures experienced a turnover rate of just 13.9%, compared to 48.4% for companies with weaker cultures. (SHRM). Cost of replacing an employee: 1.5 to 2 times that employee's salary.

In the later chapters of this book, I mention that it's not just my intuition or what a few coaches or experts are talking about; these findings are based on actual research and data on a company's culture. Suppose a survey is done and the staff members are saying a company culture is really good, or they are saying it's not good. In that case, you can see a direct influence or impact of that "feeling" on the profits of that company or how good that company is doing overall. So, it is something everyone needs to take a look at and follow, and I can't wait for everyone to implement this philosophy as much as possible because, again, it takes constant work to be successful.

Culture is a group habit, and to change any habit, it is said that you need to be doing the same thing for twenty-one days in a row, every day. I heard it takes ninety days to a year to truly build up that habit. And we are talking about just one person here. But if you want to change an entire group's habits or culture or to understand what culture actually is and how we do everything in the company, it's going to take some really strong intention and some time. If someone needs to be the leader of the company, they will want to be really intentional about that and put some rules and regulations in place for what they want to implement. Doing so makes the results visible and shows that the leaders care and the company culture is well-developed. Only then will you be able to see how your team works on their day-to-day tasks and how much ownership they feel they have.

You'll also start seeing how they feel about the company. CEO syndrome is when everyone on the team feels like the CEO, where they are able to make decisions, speak up, and feel included, seen, and heard. If all companies worked toward building a beautiful culture, then we could build a better world for all.

WORKPLACE QUESTIONS

At the end of this chapter, I want you to brainstorm a little about how the culture looks in your company. Consider the following questions:

1. How do people show up to work each day? How do you feel about your company? And while we're on the subject, what does culture mean to you?

_____

_____

_____

_____

_____

2. Were you ever an employee? Did you work at another company or for someone else? What do you remember about those times? Go back in time and think about it. If you have more than one experience, compare them. Which culture was the best you experienced? And further, which one would you call not so good? What factors made those good or not so good?

_____

_____

_____

_____

_____

As a leader whose awareness can make a real difference, this is something you can consider and implement in your company. In return, your team will reciprocate and work with you to develop a good culture in the workplace.

CHAPTER 2
CULTURE AND PROFITABILITY

"Culture eats strategy for breakfast."
~Peter Drucker, Management Consultant and Author

Throughout my journey, I have seen firsthand how the culture within an organization can dramatically influence both morale and the financial outcomes. I've seen real-life examples and experienced various leadership roles that have taught me about how culture is as crucial as any business strategy because it shapes every interaction, both within and outside the company.

The overall feeling of a workplace obviously impacts the service, the product, and the bottom line. However, it may not be so obvious to every leader or company; otherwise, we would not hear any sad stories about unsatisfactory company cultures.

The state of a company's culture comes as a direct result of how self-aware the leadership is and if they are willing to bring a change if a change is needed. I also think what needs to be said out loud—and perhaps more training on this is needed—is that leadership is trained on things like profitability, staffing, and where to cut costs, but if they look deep down at what is a truly impactful but often-overlooked area, leaders will note how their staff actually feels and what the overall company culture is. It is through such observations that they'll find a treasure trove of data that can directly affect their profits.

At this point, I think it would be a good idea to bring up some research. Personally, I wanted to prove that happy staff would provide better services, products, and overall results. To find out whether there is any research and data that backs this, I dove deeper into research about culture impacting profitability and uncovered a large amount of data.

According to a study by Deloitte,[1] the differences between companies that manage their culture proactively and those that don't are huge in many different fields. So, between the companies that manage their culture proactively and those that don't, there is a major disparity in the percentage and 30 percent higher innovation levels. Imagine your staff being just 30 percent more innovative; that's a direct impact right there when it comes to work performance or the quality of the product or ideas you're receiving.

---

1. https://www2.deloitte.com/us/en/insights/topics/innovation/corporate-innovation-program-report-and-key-takeaways.html.

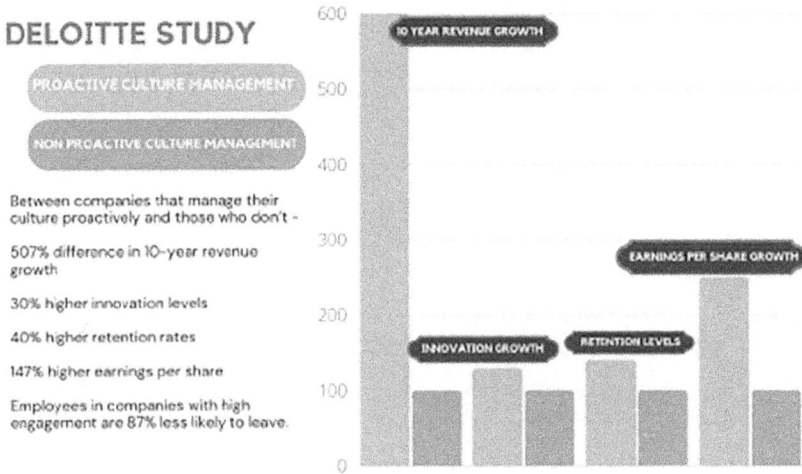

Figure 1. Deloitte study focuses on companies with proactive and non-proactive culture management strategies.[2]

We cannot overlook the 40 percent higher retention rates, nor can we look past the research from SHRM. Retention rates and getting your team to stay greatly impact bottom-line profitability. Therefore, companies that manage their culture proactively have 40 percent higher retention rates than those that don't, and the earnings are also 147 percent higher per share—a huge difference! Moreover, employees in companies with high engagement are 87 percent less likely to leave. So a gain, the importance of retention rates and the cost of replacing an employee cannot be stressed enough. All these studies show that although we may believe that a happy team member is great to have, it's very evident that this is important not only in terms of maintaining good vibes but also for productivity, creativity, commitment, and for the bottom line and overall profits.

---

2. https://www2.deloitte.com/us/en/insights/focus/human-capital-trends.html#leadership-epilogue

Enhanced performance among staff directly contributes to better business results, as well as employee retention rates. Consequently, the team develops in alignment with performance, which ultimately has a positive impact on workplace culture. In summary, a positive culture reduces turnover because hiring and training new staff is expensive.

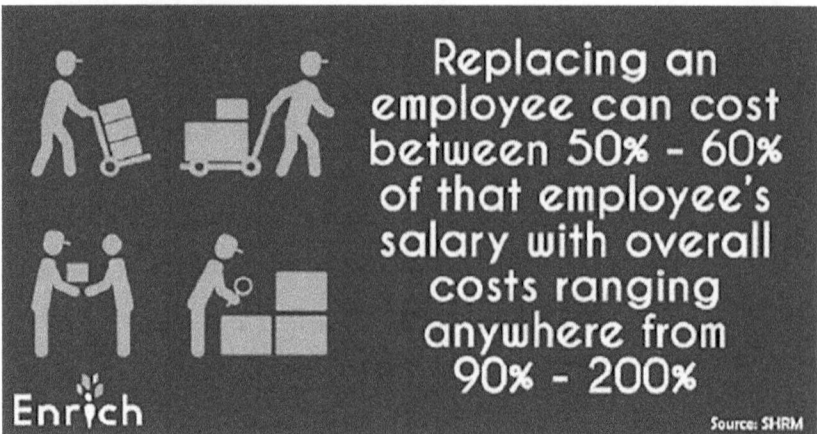

Figure 2. The cost of replacing an employee. (Source: SHRM)[3]

According to SHRM, replacing an employee can cost 50 to 60 percent of that employee's salary, with an overall cost ranging anywhere from 90 to 200 percent. This presents a large gap which, if on an ongoing basis, may not be noticeable; however, this is the gap into which the money is being drained. Hence, it is worth noting that organizations with strong cultures report lower turnover rates. The overall stability brought in by good culture, which binds the team, not only saves costs related to recruitment and training but

3. https://www.shrm.org/topics-tools/news/hr-magazine/drive-turnover

also preserves organizational knowledge and culture. Studies consistently show that companies with positive cultures exhibit higher financial performance and greater employee engagement, which largely explains why we're seeing considerable growth in the labor market, alongside increased performance, greater employee engagement, and productivity.

Another study by Gallup[4] found that companies recognize one to ten employees who have proven themselves to be highly profitable over the years spent at their respective companies. If leaders fail to intentionally pay attention to what's going on with the culture present at the workplace—the reasons why employees leave, how to retain staff, and who their highest-performing staff are—then it becomes harder to develop and improve the company as a whole. We'll discuss this further in the upcoming chapters.

Strategic Recognition Generates Employee Engagement

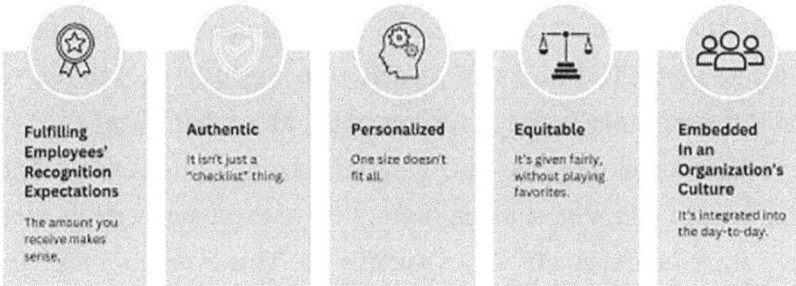

Fulfilling Employees' Recognition Expectations	Authentic	Personalized	Equitable	Embedded in an Organization's Culture
The amount you receive makes sense.	It isn't just a "checklist" thing.	One size doesn't fit all.	It's given fairly, without playing favorites.	It's integrated into the day-to-day.

---

4. https://www.gallup.com/workplace/236441/employee-recognition-low-cost-high-impact.aspx.

Figure 3. Saving on turnover costs.[5]

Directly contributing to better operational results leads to increased revenue, and a supportive culture fosters an environment where productivity can thrive. We talked about happy employees being creative and more engaged, but they're also more productive. In addition, the regenerative effect of instilling a positive internal culture extends to customer interactions. When the staff feels better, they're happier, they're feeling heard, and the overall culture is good. And then there are those who stay and do not leave. I mean, imagine a team that works for several years together, or even five or ten at the same place, truly says something about that place.

Happy employees are also good at customer interactions. And you can see that with some nurturing, they become experts in what they are, where they are, and what they do. This is because they are comfortable. What's more, satisfied employees are more likely to deliver exceptional customer service, which thus leads to higher customer satisfaction. And repeat business, just like when you have a staff that wants to come back to work every day, results in customers who want to come back to your business.

---

5. https://www.gallup.com/analytics/392540/unleashing-recognition-at-.work.aspx.

When it comes to employees' decisions to quit or stay at the company, quiet quitting, as introduced in the previous chapter, has gained prominence in recent years. So, we definitely need to talk about the impact of "quiet quitting" because it almost always goes unnoticed unless it really impacts your profits, customer service, or product quality. Unfortunately, by this time, it is usually too late. The phenomenon of quiet quitting, in which employees do the minimum required, can be detrimental to profitability. However, a strong culture combats this by engaging employees and aligning them with the company's goals. On multiple occasions, my team members in the corporate world have confided in me that they're not working for the company or the bottom line, but they work hard because what they truly wanted was to see me succeed as the leader of the project. This symbolic finding stems from the large amount of responsibilities that the leaders share in shaping the culture of the company.

However, it is, ultimately, not all about money or the company the employees work for. It really comes down to how they're feeling, why they want to succeed, and why they want to perform better in a certain project. Employees are often there in presence only and perhaps feel disgruntled about an aspect of their role or the company itself. This speaks a lot about the culture, where they may not feel able to speak up or discuss what's concerning them. As a result, their performance slowly decreases, and you may not even see it until it becomes clear the employee is "quiet quitting." I often wonder whether the leaders have been proactive and intentional about the culture they aim to foster. If so, then they can catch "quiet quitters" pretty early and avoid having them in their teams.

A great way to prevent something like quiet quitting is being intentional about maintaining open communication throughout the company. At the end of the day, what matters the most is how much you care as a leader. If you care, you'll see those signs. Given the impact that quiet quitting can have on employee and team performance, it should always be considered when looking at how profitable the company culture is over time.

WORKSHEET

The Profit Formula

This simple formula, which shows how profit impact is equal to increased productivity value plus retention cost savings plus customer loyalty revenue increase, helps businesses and leaders quantify the financial impact of culture directly, making the benefits tangible and actionable.

**(Increased Productivity Value) +
(Retention Cost Savings) +
(Customer Loyalty Revenue Increase) =**

Profit Impact

Figure 4. The Profit Formula.

CHAPTER 3
DEFINING GOOD CULTURE

"Clients do not come first. Employees come first.
If you take care of your employees,
they will take care of the clients."
~Richard Branson

n the above quote, Marklin reminds us of the deep emotional and psychological impact our work environment has on us. This perspective shifts our understanding of culture from a set of policies or rules to the very atmosphere that surrounds us every day at work. Good culture is about experiencing the heartbeat of an organization. How do we really feel about our workplace?

"Culture is how employees' hearts and stomachs feel about
Monday morning on Sunday night."
~Bill Marklin

This should come as a reminder that culture is not just about the rules we follow, but the feelings we experience as a part of our work community. This is a good perspective to utilize when we want to define a good culture.

If we try to envision the ideal culture, imagine a workplace where everyone feels as empowered as the CEO. This is the hallmark of a truly transformative culture, a place where each person is deeply invested in their work and feels like an integral part of the company's mission. Achieving this in any organization requires more than just good intentions; it goes to the root level of the company.

Instilling the ideal culture requires deliberate actions and commitments from all, especially those in leadership. Such an environment is built on mutual respect and shared goals, creating a sense of ownership and pride in all aspects of work.

LEADERSHIP

Leadership is the guiding star of any workplace. The behavior and integrity of leaders set the tone for everyone. A leader's action speaks volumes; therefore, if a leader shows their team that they value honesty and transparency, their example will set a standard and build a foundation of trust that permeates the entire organization. As a result, the team will mirror what they see in the leader. And when leaders act ethically and openly, they set a tone of trust and reliability that supports a positive work environment.

Leadership is the first element of a good culture. It is so integral to culture because that's where everything starts.

"Everything rises and falls on Leadership.
And that leadership is influence—
nothing more, nothing less."
~John Maxwell

So, I'd say that good leadership is the most important component of a good culture because that is where the thought process starts. We discussed the importance of profitability in the previous chapter. It is essential that leaders understand that the culture is the personality of their business; therefore, they must have the intention to build it.

You know, leaders are those who invest in culture mentally, financially, and physically, so that's something that starts from them. The very first point to consider is that leadership is the guiding star for a good culture at a workplace. Now, let's take a look at some other aspects.

PURPOSE

What makes a good culture? I think another important element of a good culture is purpose. If the company and leadership are purposeful, they have a clear, well-defined purpose and vision that they practice on a daily basis. The leaders live that purpose and vision.

And if this purpose and vision resonate with the staff, then it will be the fuel that drives them, that just builds them up from the inside out. This fuel is called *intrinsic motivation,* as Daniel Pink calls it, which plays a greater role than any form of extrinsic motivation, such as financial incentives. When your work resonates, when your team resonates with the meaning, every task forms part of the bigger picture. In a workplace in which you know the leader, CEO, or leadership team and are clear about the vision they have for their team, individual efforts contribute to the organization's goals. As a result, employees are clear about what they're doing and what they are working toward. Therefore, aligning personal ambitions with company purpose creates a work environment that is not just fulfilling but also exciting and motivating.

COMMUNICATION

Another essential component of culture is good and transparent communication. Open lines of communication are essential for any kind of connection or relationship, whether personal or professional. Creating an open environment where everyone feels safe to express their ideas, share their concerns, and provide feedback prevents many issues from escalating and cultivates a sense of safety and belonging.

Cultivating a sense of safety and belonging is crucial to developing a thriving culture. That's one very important part where leadership comes in. We talked about purpose in order for them to communicate. So, it is important that leadership communicates the purpose of the company, what they stand for, and what their expectations are to their team as clearly as possible. Then, they should be open to feedback and provide that safe space.

In that kind of atmosphere, the team feels good coming to work every day because they feel seen and heard, and it's all about communication.

DIVERSITY AND INCLUSION

Diversity and inclusion mean celebrating every voice. Diversity is having a mixed team from different backgrounds that enriches our workplace by bringing a variety of perspectives to the table, enhancing creativity, and improving decision-making processes. So, diversity is an amazing way to add more color and dynamism to the culture.

And diversity definitely adds to the bottom line when a team brings all these different experiences, thoughts, and opinions to the table. Going back to communication, when you feel everyone is included, inclusion forms a large part of the team's security. It's about more than meeting the quotas or a certain percentage of a certain experience or background; it's about creating a space where everyone, regardless of their background, feels genuinely valued and understood. Such is the importance of inclusion. I know we are going into many elements here, but they all go hand in hand with each other.

For diversity and inclusion to be successful, leadership requires a comprehensive, deep-rooted understanding, along with strong communication skills. Again, feedback is necessary.

- How is your team feeling?
- Are they feeling included?
- Are they feeling left out?

AN ENVIRONMENT OF GROWTH

The next aspect I would like to mention is creating an environment of growth, where leadership builds pathways and cares about their team's growth and future. When leaders are concerned and care about the company's bottom line, they see their team as a closely knit group of human beings who are there to learn and grow. A leader's experience is also crucial to the team, which can lead to a more personalized style of leadership where every team member feels like they're seen and heard and that the company cares about them.

When leaders show their team that they are invested in their future by providing opportunities for growth, whether through training, mentorship, or clear career paths, investment in team development is an investment in the health and future of their entire organization, as well as the team members. Assessing where everyone is, meeting them there, providing opportunities for one-on-one feedback and opportunities for teams to let the leadership know where they see themselves in a few years, and being intentional about the strengths of staff and leadership alike sets the groundwork to build a personalized growth or education plan. I mean, there is just so much that can be done, and I can only imagine a culture where everyone at the company wants to stay, learn, and grow, building and rising together. When new team members join the organization, they notice how the team members have been there for so long and learned so much. This is a great indicator of a good culture.

POSITIVE VIBES: RECOGNITION AND APPRECIATION

A workplace where there are no opportunities to recognize and appreciate our mistakes further adds to the positivity of the environment. This workplace has mastered the art of appreciation. I'll be here, where all the personal achievements of the team are recognized and celebrated. Timely, specific recognition aligned with the company's values makes people feel valued and motivates them to keep striving for excellence. Some good words and kind words can be all it takes, but giving feedback on an employee's accomplishments, small or large, will really motivate them to keep doing more and go above and beyond to achieve success. Whether through formal awards or informal acknowledgments, feeling appreciated for our contributions reinforces our value to the team.

Leadership can write a list to record where and when they demonstrated intentional behavior, and this can also be done intentionally. An "employee of the month" award is a great example of this, and it should be set in place as a rule and regulation. This way, it is never missed. There are many other traditions that can be put in place to avoid missing out on an opportunity to recognize team effort.

A COLLABORATIVE ENVIRONMENT

Another great part of a good culture is collaboration, where leadership encourages teamwork rather than, you know, working in silos. There are tasks that only require one-on-one work or one person working on them, but together, we can achieve more. Therefore, any task a team can work together on is a great way to build up a company's culture. For example, in my business, the teachers or staff were assigned to one room— their individual classrooms; there was no way for them to connect other than if they happened to be in the break room at the same time, which was hard because every break was at a different hour. To feel a part of something bigger, it was a great idea to have them collaborate on a project.

There are forty other people working here on any given team-building activity, even in environments where they don't usually see each other. This builds team morale considerably. A workplace where a culture of teamwork is fostered through common goals and a collaborative environment that enhances our work experience by allowing us to combine our diverse strengths and knowledge not only makes challenges easier to manage but also builds a strong sense of community and shared purpose. A few years back, I heard that loneliness is the biggest pandemic. I hear that a lot from people who work from home. There is not much connection, they're burned out, and they're not meeting up with friends. Knowing this, workplaces and leadership share the responsibility of creating these communities around collaborative work.

With a strong purpose and vision, along with good communication and daily teamwork, employees develop a sense of unity and feel better overall, both mentally and physically. This is the ripple effect of good leadership and the intention to develop a good culture in the workplace.

WORK-LIFE HARMONY

Work-life harmony is closely connected to good culture. Going back to the topic of staff mental health, I say that the brain is everything. Even if there have been days when I'm sitting at my chair, working from home the whole day, and have not moved from my chair for several hours, at the end of the day, I still sometimes feel exhausted, depending on how the day went. This tells us that our mind consumes a lot of energy.

Imagine a good workplace where the leadership cares about your work-life harmony and where there is a healthy balance between professional and personal lives and needs. Work-life harmony is crucial for everyone to feel good.

Flexible working conditions and understanding personal needs can sometimes boost employee performance and morale when they can't focus at work. In such situations, there's no reason to keep them at work if they can accomplish more at home. Making this judgment goes back to communication, where the staff member, the team member, feels comfortable sharing that need with the leadership and requesting that flexibility. In turn, the leadership places their trust in their staff in the knowledge that even if they have that flexibility, the team member will be more productive when they're able to cater to their personal needs and also work at the same time.

In parallel with flexible work arrangements and understanding personal needs, ensuring ample time for rest and recreation will help maintain a vibrant and productive team. It is helpful to stay productive and happy, both at work and at home, so I think this is an important area for leaders. Doing so shows that both the leadership and the company really care about their employees. You know, I always say, and I might say several times over, that when leadership cares, the team cares about the leadership in turn.

ENCOURAGING INNOVATION

Empowering teams to innovate and cultivating a thriving environment of innovation requires allowing an ample sense of freedom. In a team comprising various backgrounds and experiences, we let them innovate. We let them come up with new ideas. They're free to innovate. This is not a command-and-control type of environment or culture; it's adaptive, it's agile, and the team is encouraged to innovate. Such an environment is not only motivating and inspiring, but it also pushes us to think creatively and enjoy our interactions, making each day at work more fulfilling and exciting.

The workplace should be a source of inspiration, innovation, and joy, not just a place to work, but a place where the team members are able to be themselves. Freedom in the workplace is another aspect that contributes to a good work culture. The above are just a few examples of successful leadership.

Building a great culture takes a group of people with a lot of positivity, which is, again, a group habit. If it looks different right now, it is going to take a lot of work, even if some things are already in place. So, positivity is a great first step.

And then, if you wish to see change, it will take some work to change. It will require the leadership to set some rules and regulations, as well as some expectations from themselves, and being intentional about it is a great first step.

WORKPLACE QUESTIONS

1. Question one provides some reflective insight for leaders. What environments have enabled you to thrive? What leadership qualities inspired you? Use these insights to envision the type of culture you want to nurture in your company.

_____

_____

_____

_____

_____

2. Question two focuses on practical implementation. If you are in a leadership position, see this chapter as a personal call to action. Look at your current workplace culture. What could be improved? Note them down, and take deliberate steps to cultivate a healthier, more engaging environment.

_____

_____

_____

_____

_____

Through thoughtful exploration and implementation of these principles, you can create a workplace where culture is not just an abstract concept, but a living, breathing part of everyday life, where every Monday is a welcome opportunity, and every team member feels like a vital part of something great. Employees should want to come to work every day and be excited about it.

CHAPTER 4
THE ROLE OF LEADERSHIP

Figure 5. Culture versus Strategy.[1]

n this chapter, I want to talk about inspirational leadership and how that transforms company culture. There is a great saying, "Culture eats strategy for breakfast." (a quote by management consultant and writer Peter Drucker). I love that because no matter

---

1. https://x.com/FerraroRoberto/status/1552153756711751681.

how strong a company's strategic plan might be, the culture within the organization is what ultimately defines or determines its success. This is highlighted in numerous research studies, personal experiences, and accounts from people in the corporate world. The wealth of reports clearly indicate the role that a leader has in creating a positive and effective culture that not only aligns with but also accelerates the company's strategic goals because the leader is the one who defines the strategy for everything, from numbers to group habits.

Leaders set the tone and expectations for behavior, actions, and decisions within the company on a day-to-day basis. Leaders should model behaviors that reflect not only their values but also the company that they're running, including its values and influence, which, in turn, influence employee interaction and behavior. As people do what they see, effective leaders inspire the day-to-day activities of their company, instilling trust and motivation in an environment where, depending on the leader, the level of innovation and cooperation is what drives the company forward.

Without strong leadership, a company risks developing a negative culture or disjointed culture, which will then lead to decreased employee engagement. This leads to a negative cycle of lower productivity and labor retention issues. In essence, leaders are the builders or architects of their organizations. What they want to achieve with the company and how they demonstrate their motivation directly shape the daily workplace environment. This is how we define culture, which defines long-term success.

I note the successes of visionary leaders and the impact they have had on their companies or organizations. We read about it all the time: a certain change they brought to the company that caused it to thrive and gain recognition. There is no limit to what a leader can do to their organization through their vision.

It is as if they set their mind on something. I think that's the key to building a culture that has no limits. If they set their mind on something, they can definitely achieve it. The following part of the chapter looks at several leaders' actions and philosophies and how we can learn from them to gain valuable insight into building a culture that fosters engagement, purpose, and sustainable success.

ANN MULCAHY: XEROX

I am fascinated by how Ann Mulcahy led Xerox from the moment she joined as CEO. Xerox was at the point of losing it all. When Mulcahy came on board, she faced that monumental challenge. The company was going bankrupt, and her approach to the company's crisis provided a masterclass in crisis leadership and organizational turnaround. One of the most important aspects she worked on was transparency and trust.

> *"Employees who believe that management is concerned*
> *about them as a whole person—not just an employee—*
> *are more productive, more satisfied, more fulfilled.*
> *Satisfied employees mean satisfied customers,*
> *which leads to profitability."*
> ~Anne Mulcahy

Mulcahy emphasized that there would be a transfer and communication. She openly shared the company's financial state and recovery, her current position in the company, and what she planned to do. She shared her ideas with her employees, and this transparency generated trust. When you get to know your employees, you are able to earn their trust. They are committed to working on your vision of turning the company around.

Mulcahy traveled throughout the world to meet with employees and clients, particularly to work on engagement and inclusion. She traveled extensively to meet all the stakeholders worldwide and discuss their ideas and concerns.

Ann Mulcahy's story highlights the value that open communication and inclusion bring to an organization. This form of direct engagement, where a CEO asked the employees questions and requested feedback, made the employees feel valued and created a collaborative atmosphere where employees were welcome to innovate. Under Mulcahy's leadership, Xerox underwent a cultural transformation and reset that prioritized customer service and operational efficiency. Her development of a good culture at a grassroots level with a specific focus on customer service became one of the company's core values and helped to restore Xerox's market position. This turnaround is a great example of transformative leadership.

HOWARD SCHULTZ: STARBUCKS

Next, I want to talk about Howard Schultz. Starbucks is one of my favorite places to go just about every day, and I just love to see warm smiles from all the staff. After my second or third visit at any Starbucks, they would remember my name and my order. It never fails to surprise me. I don't know how many daily customers Starbucks receives, but I bet they do that for everybody. Always happy. So there is something at play there.

"Profitability is a shallow goal if it doesn't have a real purpose. The purpose has to be to share the profits with others."
~Howard Schultz

Howard Schultz, the founder and CEO of Starbucks, has been with the company for decades now, and his leadership has been marked by his commitment to equity, community engagement, and social responsibility. I have heard so much about the ethical sourcing of their beans. That's kind of what brings up the social responsibility part.

Community engagement also marks Howard Schultz's reign at Starbucks. I've always seen those boards up there, which you will see at a local café, to encourage all the local businesses. Starbucks encourages that. There is also a huge focus on their employees or staff and providing them with opportunities to develop. I've heard about Starbucks introducing health benefits, such as health insurance for all part-time and full-time employees. That is very rare in the retail sector. Schultz also initiated college tuition coverage through the Starbucks College achievement plan, which improves employee satisfaction, as well as loyalty and productivity, because Starbucks employees know their leader cares about them.

Another amazing thing about Starbucks is that they offer stock options, called Beanstalk, to the staff. I love the creativity there. As stockholders, employees are referred to as partners. Howard Schultz's leadership helps them feel more connected to the company's success because if the company succeeds, the employee succeeds. In turn, the employee will work harder for the company's success because they are partners, not employees. Fostering a sense of ownership and pride in their work also proves Starbucks' commitment to offering equity and ownership to its teams. As a result, more people want to work at Starbucks, which reduces turnover while creating a more motivated, productive, and positive workforce with overall great customer service and sourcing.

Schultz also set up many social initiatives, such as the Race Together campaign, which tackles pressing social issues through its commitment to social justice and open dialogue. He is also passionate about environmental stewardship and social impact programs.

> *"Companies should not have a singular view of profitability. There needs to be a balance between commerce and social responsibility... The companies that are authentic about it will wind up as the companies that make more money."*
> ~Howard Schultz

One of Schultz's greatest achievements was his ability to enhance brand image and attract customers and employees in alignment with the company's values, such as ethical consumption and social awareness. Howard Schultz is a leader who takes the initiative and knows the impact they can make.

Imagine the ripple effect of that great leadership. I've also read a lot about the culture of inclusion implemented at Starbucks and the company's focus on diversity and inclusion. Starbucks' employees, who are hired from differing backgrounds, feel welcomed and valued. This contributes to a rich and inclusive culture that allows for positive staff-customer interaction. Howard Schultz's contribution to the culture at Starbucks is a great example of leadership. And we can see how successful Starbucks has become. It's not a one-day turnaround; it's the creation and building of a great culture from the ground up, and it takes a visionary leader like Howard Schultz, who saw what he could start and where it could go.

INDRA NOOYI: PEPSICO

Indra Nooyi was the CEO of PepsiCo. I've heard such great things about her. She's of Indian origin, and I was born and raised in India, too. She caught my eye when she was announced as the CEO of PepsiCo, and I instantly wanted to learn all about her. After reading her biography, I got to know where she grew up. I have been there, and that story is close to my heart. I learned a lot from her story and attended her masterclass on the Masterclass app. I highly recommend it.

"It's our job to draw the best out of everyone. That means employees must be able to immerse their whole selves in a work environment in which they can develop their careers, families, and philanthropy, and truly believe they are cared for."
~Indira Nooyi

Nooyi's time at PepsiCo was characterized by her drive to integrate purpose with business performance, which ultimately led to significant cultural shifts within the company. Indra Nooyi's tenure redefined corporate success for PepsiCo. Profitability should not come at the expense of sustainability and health. Under her leadership, PepsiCo expanded its product line to include healthier options. This is a great example of leadership being intentional about performance with purpose.

Indra Nooyi's story shows how she changed a company for good. She was able to do that because she was at the top and had the ability to change the culture from the ground up. Nooyi is known for championing a culture of innovation that always encourages new ideas and initiatives. Not only did she respond to market trends, but she also anticipated them, keeping PepsiCo ahead of industry curves. I've heard interesting stories about her visiting different grocery stores and talking to her team about how their snacks are stored in the grocery stores. She truly believes in innovation and encourages innovative ideas.

She's also known to empower her employees by aligning the company's objectives with broader social goals. This is something any leader can always work on. The above examples highlight how setting solid ground rules of innovation and employee empowerment fosters a culture of innovation and empowerment of employees.

TONY HSIEH: ZAPPOS

Tony Hsieh, the CEO of Zappos, is recognized for creating a culture of service and happiness. His leadership style is a good example of how unconventional approaches to management leadership and culture can yield extraordinary results when the intention is good.

> *"At Zappos, we really view culture as our No. 1 priority.*
> *We decided that if we get the culture right, most of the stuff,*
> *like building a brand around delivering the very best*
> *customer service, will just take care of itself."*
> ~Tony Hsieh, *New York Times*

One of Tony Hsieh's most unconventional ideas I have heard about is a flat organizational culture or structure where the layers of management are removed. Though challenging to put into practice, Tony Hsieh managed to do so, and his example set a precedent for several other companies to follow suit. Hsieh's employee-centric policy facilitated open communication and quicker decision-making, where everybody has a say in all decisions.

Another unconventional rule or policy is the famous quitting bonus, which he offered to new hires who decided that Zappos was not the right fit for them. His unique policy speaks volumes about the company's commitment to ensuring that its employees are truly happy and aligned with the company culture.

Customer connection, which emphasizes customer service and personal connection, is another hallmark of Zappos. This quality separates them from their competitors and has helped the company build a strong sense of customer loyalty to the brand.

The above examples can help you identify leaders in our lives, even those in the companies where we work or have worked. Do you remember a leader's name or someone you saw who has made a tremendous impact and established grassroots-level policies to show the world that leadership is integral in shaping good company culture?

To conclude this chapter, I would like to offer some point-based worksheets with reflective, open-ended questions.

WORKPLACE QUESTIONS

1. Question one looks at defining cultural traits. Identify five cultural traits you wish to embed or bring into your company. Some examples include transparency, inclusivity, social responsibility, and employee engagement. What would you like to see?

_____

_____

_____

_____

_____

2. Question two focuses on how we implement those traits. For each cultural trait, I would encourage you to develop specifications and define what changes are needed. Let's start by listing some specific actions, such as policies. What kind of communication strategies do you adopt?

_____

_____

_____

_____

_____

3. Can you provide your staff with any training to encourage transparency? I think about the importance of feedback. How can we create mechanisms for ongoing feedback from employees? Any suggestions?

_____

_____

_____

_____

_____

Ask for employees' viewpoints and any other ideas about what they would like to see, or what kind of adjustments they would like to be made. Doing so will help maintain a dynamic culture that can adapt to both internal and external changes. By integrating these insights and strategies, it's clear when a leader is intentional. You can then embark on your vision to transform and refine your company's culture. In turn, your staff will be happy, and your company will be rewarded with success.

CHAPTER 5
CULTIVATING OWNERSHIP AND PURPOSE

"When people are financially invested, they want a return.
When people are emotionally invested, they want to contribute."
~Simon Sinek

E stablishing a culture where every staff member feels like they own the company or that they are a partner is a great achievement. I go back to the time when I owned a business and was able to generate that feeling I saw in almost all my employees. I was truly proud of that.

My employees were equally proud of their work and being a part of the company. And that is such a great state to reach because you no longer need to worry about the company's success. You have a team there who cares about your vision, and they are there to achieve that. They know that what they are working toward will bring success and good health to the company. And that, in turn, is their partnership, too.

In our journey through organizational culture and leadership, we arrive at a fundamental truth that the ability to cultivate a sense of ownership in the team members is quintessential for business success. If an employee goes to work solely for their paycheck, then, believe me, their whole heart is not in the work.

In this chapter, I want to dive deeper into these areas of ownership and purpose and how we can achieve it so that all the team members feel that way.

Ownership is not just a business concept; it represents a mindset that should be present at every level of an organization or company. It most definitely begins with leaders who truly care, embody the principles of ownership, and encourage their teams to follow them. By demonstrating a personal commitment to every part of their work, leaders can inspire their teams to take on every task and challenge with a sense of personal investment and pride.

I bet everyone has those stories about their career journey. I remember a great story about making decisions. So many stories are related to the trash can, but I think this one comes down to the day-to-day functioning of a company—the daily routine or schedule.

THE TRASH CAN STORY

Cleanliness and hygiene form an integral part of any organization or company. Some employees do not always feel it is their responsibility to keep the surroundings clean. Rather, they do merely what is written in their contract. However, there are those who go above and beyond. It is their dedica-

tion and behavior that make them real partners in the company. They're not just employees; they're not just there to get a paycheck. So, imagine walking down a company hallway and noticing a piece of trash lying next to the bin. What do you do?

You can pick it up and throw it into the trash, or you can leave it there and wait for the cleaners to come in and pick it up. So, it's just one small decision. If you look at it that way, it's actually the sentiment the employee has toward the company. That's what comes into play. That simple act exemplifies how taking initiative, regardless of one's role or job description, is fundamental to building an ownership culture.

I think no discussion of organizational ownership would be complete without examining the model at Disney. I hear so many stories about Disney that every employee—from the characters in costume to the managers—knows exactly what to do. When you ask them, they will know the answer to your question and will be very polite when telling you about it. That's what creates the whole environment at Disney. Every employee, whether they're a janitor or a senior executive, is encouraged to take company ownership in that environment. They make sure that every guest experiences nothing short of magic, which stems directly from these staff members, who feel genuinely responsible for the company's brand and the satisfaction of its visitors. What we see in the long run in these companies is a great return in the form of happy customers.

There's a lot to learn from how Disney instills these values and the impact the company has on both employee satisfaction and customer experience.

As an employee progresses through their careers, there are periods between promotions that can often lead to a sense of aimlessness or lost purpose. It is during those periods when we can learn more about how we can inculcate that sense of purpose in them. It is at that moment when it becomes necessary to stimulate that feeling or sentiment of ownership and purpose. A strong and purpose-driven culture within a company will support continuous engagement and motivation.

Millennials and Gen Z are more likely to take job decisions based on purpose

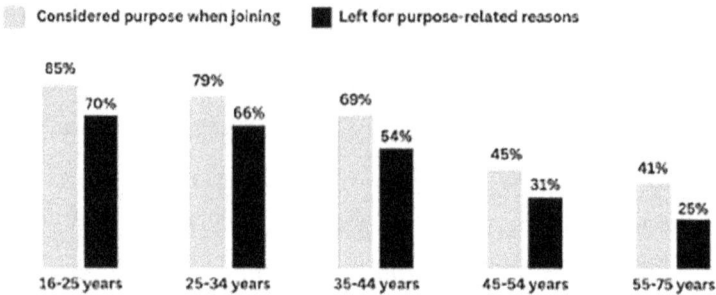

Considered purpose when joining ▪ Left for purpose-related reasons

85%	79%	69%	45%	41%
70%	66%	54%	31%	25%
16-25 years	25-34 years	35-44 years	45-54 years	55-75 years

Figure 6. Job decisions among Millennials and Gen Z. Deloitte Insights.[1]

---

1. [1]   https://www2.deloitte.com/us/en/insights/topics/strategy/mind-the-purpose-gap.html

Leaders must align the employee's personal growth with the organization's greater goals. By doing so, companies can ensure that staff feel valued and understood throughout their professional journey. In turn, this will help leaders maintain high levels of engagement and reduce turnover. In addition to the positive impact happiness has on the workplace, research also tells us a lot about the impact of a purpose-driven workplace.

Purpose ranks higher on senior managers' agenda than on those of middle managers and non-managerial employees

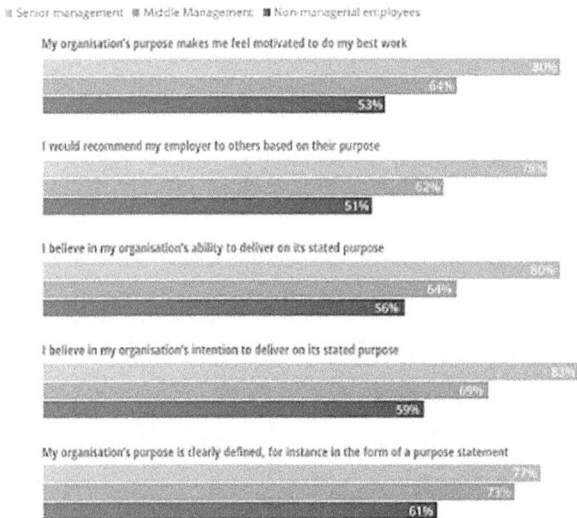

Senior management ▪ Middle Management ▪ Non-managerial employees

My organisation's purpose makes me feel motivated to do my best work
80%
64%
53%

I would recommend my employer to others based on their purpose
78%
62%
51%

I believe in my organisation's ability to deliver on its stated purpose
80%
64%
56%

I believe in my organisation's intention to deliver on its stated purpose
83%
69%
59%

My organisation's purpose is clearly defined, for instance in the form of a purpose statement
77%
73%
61%

Source: Deloitte analysis, 2022.

Deloitte Insights | deloitte.com/insights

Figure 7. Purpose as a key factor for senior management.
(Deloitte Insights)[2]

---

2. http://www.deloitte.com/insights

Employees at companies that care about their purpose and vision are significantly more engaged than their competitors, and even more so with a culture that promotes open communication. Research shows that 73 percent of workers at purpose-centric organizations report greater job satisfaction and engagement. That is a significant number. With greater job satisfaction comes higher performance and, consequently, more loyalty to the organization.

Purpose is a critical component of workplace culture. But how can we connect the team member or staff member with the company's mission and values? Because it's not just beneficial; it's essential for the culture of ownership. The employees need to see and feel why they're there, along with the importance and relevance of their work within the larger framework of the company's goals and objectives. Whether a large or small company, an employee comes to work every day, nine to five. They have a job description or a set of duties, and imagine that being a mechanical, transactional give-and-take. Compare that to what happens when the employee feels truly connected to the company's mission. It is important to effectively communicate and embody the company's missions and daily activities, perhaps through emails, flyers, something that consistently details meetings and training on the company's mission and values. It is also important to ensure that it resonates deeply with every team member, from top to bottom. How do we implement that? There are many different ways to promote such an environment.

Now is a good moment to reflect on the tangible and intangible benefits of cultivating a culture of ownership and purpose. There are some actionable items we can add here. First, leaders should assess the company's progress and current state, as well as the leadership itself. Getting this information starts with obtaining feedback. An anonymous feedback box is useful for such a task.

- Where is your staff right now?
- How do they feel?
- What's the sentiment?
- What do they think of the leadership and the CEO of the company or leadership team?

A lot of self-reflection and self-awareness regarding how your own behavior as a leader promotes a sense of ownership among team members can help during this process. Regularly demonstrating commitment to the company's goals and values in your daily actions and decisions is a strong characteristic of leadership, as is the ability to communicate the big picture. Therefore, it is important to ensure that every team member understands how their individual role contributes to the broader company mission. It is important to remember is that the role of the individual contributes to the broader company mission. Regular meetings, newsletters, and updates to talk about the company's goals and achievements keep employees informed. Another step can be to encourage any kind of innovation and initiative among employees.

Further, rewarding employees who take proactive steps to solve problems and improve processes can be a stepping stone to achieving a sense of ownership because it shows how they are able to take decisions, be a part of a decision, or give their own suggestions on how to do a certain thing, and then seeing that happen in real-time. A great example in my company was creating a wall of fame, a recognition program to highlight moments where someone really took ownership.

Once a week, we would recognize an employee who took ownership related to a task. Employees could rate staff members if they saw them doing something good, going above and beyond to provide help or support, or any time they showed an act of ownership. Further, and as I reinforce in every chapter, implementing open communication channels is key.

We often hear that communication is everything. It is through communication that we learn how we are doing as leaders. A leader who has continuous one-on-one calls and team meetings while being observant and attending regular forums where employees can voice their ideas and concerns will have a good understanding of their impact on not only the employees and but the company as a whole.

Employees should be able to talk about their concerns or new ideas, but they also need to feel genuinely heard by the management. Leaders can give employees opportunities, but also take action to demonstrate care and that their voices are being heard. They should also encourage teamwork and the feeling of being a part of something bigger, such as in cross-departmental meetings.

Giving employees a voice and a platform encourages broader understanding and even greater teamwork by instilling the feeling of being a part of a team. Promoting continuous learning through training and development opportunities further empowers employees to take on new challenges, responsibilities, and opportunities for mentorship. This practice indicates to the staff that you— as leadership—know they are an integral part of the company, and they have a strong feeling of ownership. Also, make sure the individual goals and organizational objectives are aligned, conduct performance reviews, help your team members set personal goals that align with the company's mission, and use these alignments as stepping stones or touch points for recognizing and rewarding employee achievements. Whether the individual or the company, the team should feel the same as the company—that they're growing with the company.

Giving the employees the power to set their own benchmarks for success and holding them accountable for reaching this target fosters an environment where both, successful or not, can openly discuss opportunities for learning. Gradually increasing the level of autonomy gives power to the employees as they demonstrate their ability to handle more responsibility. Recognize them, reward them, and encourage teams to lead projects or tasks with minimal supervision to boost their confidence and greater feelings of ownership.

These are just a few practical steps that can be taken to inculcate a feeling of ownership and purpose. And when the whole staff, the whole team, works as if they are partners in the company, then nothing can stop the company from succeeding.

WORKPLACE QUESTIONS

How Will Your Staff Rate Your Company Culture (High, Medium, Low, and Why?):

1. How will your staff rate your overall Company Culture?

_____

_____

_____

_____

_____

2. How will they rate your Leadership?

_____
_____
_____
_____
_____

3. How will they rate the Workplace Atmosphere?

_____
_____
_____
_____
_____

4. How will they rate Training & Growth opportunities?

_____
_____
_____
_____
_____

5. How will your staff rate Diversity & Inclusion at your Center?

_____

_____

_____

_____

_____

6. How will your staff rate the effectiveness of Communication within your team?

_____

_____

_____

_____

_____

7. How will your staff rate being Recognized and Appreciated for their contributions?

_____

_____

_____

_____

_____

8. How will they rate how effectively the company handles change?

_____

_____

_____

_____

_____

9. How will they rate the sense of Community?

_____

_____

_____

_____

_____

10. Final Reflection: What other feedback would they have?

_____

_____

_____

_____

_____

CHAPTER 6
COMMUNICATION, INCLUSIVITY, AND DIVERSITY

"Diversity is being invited to the party;
inclusion is being asked to dance."
~Verna Myers

An integral part of a great culture is inclusivity and diversity. There is a lot to mention here, but I'll try to focus on a few aspects that truly resonate with me. Inclusivity and diversity intertwine to create a robust and resilient company or organization.

I want to dive deeper into the transformative power of creating an environment where every voice is heard and valued. This is something I have personally felt so often during my career, my entrepreneurship journey, my leadership journey, and my time with the corporate world.

Very early on in my career, I learned that the cornerstone for any and every successful team is the ability to communicate openly and honestly. How much can we say in the workplace? Even if we say something, how much is heard or acted upon? Communication affects everything from team dynamics to individual performance, so freedom of speech makes all the difference when it comes to company performance.

In one of my very first leadership positions, I saw how teams would get together in environments in which everyone has been given an opportunity to talk. It's all about that little change where they have the opportunity to speak. In such meetings, the leader would facilitate the meeting, ask for updates, and then tell the team what needs to be done. However, team members did not have the opportunity to really speak up and talk about where they were, what their needs were, or what kind of support they needed.

I started a biweekly meeting where everyone would get a turn to speak. I considered this a transformative moment to bring the team together to generate new and innovative and stimulate some deep, meaningful conversations. The well-attended meetings provided much clarity and direction and transformed the typical anxiety associated with meetings and employee evaluations and assessments.

In addition to biweekly meetings, another great activity to open up communication is performance evaluation, which, in my opinion, should be a regular and anticipated interaction conducted in a comfortable environment for all employees.

I suggest conducting these performance evaluations either monthly or once every six months. I have always enjoyed conducting one-on-one and group feedback sessions as they never fail to bring up useful information that can be hard to obtain on a day-to-day basis. Imagine the kind of productivity and efficiency that would be generated if leaders and teams could touch base with each other regularly. Feedback sessions should never be like a monologue, but rather a dialogue where both parties are able to share their feelings. Leaders should not tell staff members how they're doing; instead, they should encourage the staff members to state their current feelings and aspirations while reassuring them that their voices are being heard.

Reassuring staff really goes a long way and has direct results. For example, if a staff member mentions a training session they would like to attend, the conversation should not end in a one-on-one performance evaluation but could also result in the leader scheduling or providing that training program. This not only helps to clarify expectations and responsibilities but also creates an environment where the team members feel safe to express any concerns, new ideas, or requests. While performance evaluations are commonplace, I do not feel they are conducted enough. Evaluations should be ongoing and on a frequent basis.

A range of feedback mechanisms further aid communication in the workplace. I already mentioned the anonymous feedback box, which I introduced to my company. Early on, the staff was not used to it, but I kept reminding them to use it because I really wanted to know how they felt, and I wanted to improve their work-life harmony if I could. Ultimately, the anonymous feedback box allowed the staff members, many of whom hesitated to speak up in meetings, to provide written feedback anonymously. The anonymous feedback box is just a very simple tool that can significantly enhance communication for those more comfortable presenting their insights in writing. In my experience with my own employees, I feel that it shows you have an existing culture in the workplace that values every voice. You also recognize that feedback is not a threat, but an opportunity to grow. This is just one example of how feedback can be requested, but it also reinforces employees' right to speak their minds in meetings, even with a simple show of hands. You can always tell your employees that they are welcome to reach out at any time by email, but you must remember to follow up with all the feedback.

The topic of feedback brings me to the significance of accessibility to leaders. Leadership must be approachable for communication to function. If we want to maintain open and ongoing communication, leaders must make themselves available and reassure staff that if they want to reach out to you or any level of management and leadership, they will feel more connected and committed to the organization's mission. Many studies have shown that when employees feel that their voices are heard, they are four times more likely to feel empowered to perform their best. That's a huge number. So, that's an important part leaders need to remember.

Another great way to maintain open communication, transparency, and inclusivity is keeping staff members informed about where the company is going and how the company is doing financially. As staff know the leaders are wholly invested in the company, they are more motivated to achieve company goals and align with its vision. T rust is created and their belief is reinforced in the company, the leaders, and transparency about metrics and salaries. Clarifying salaries across the various roles in the company directly impacts morale and trust in the company. This is another example of financial transparency and inclusivity where companies post salaries in job posts to avoid any confusion as to who is paid what.

Leaders who truly care about their company boost employees' trust and belief in leaders' awareness of staff needs. Whatever they can see, they can afford to add to their company benefits, which meets the diverse needs of the staff. This includes physical accommodations, like pumping rooms for new mothers, prayer or meditation rooms, or even a quiet room for de-stressing, taking a nap, or just to decompress. These types of spaces are critical in supporting a diverse range of employee needs and indicate to the staff that their personal needs and comfort are valued by the leadership and that satisfying those needs can increase job satisfaction and productivity.

In light of what we have learned from this chapter, it is clear that diversity and inclusion have a considerable impact on workplace culture. It is not solely about making the staff feel better and in a place that they belong to, but rather something to apply as a model to the entire business structure. We must also remember that companies that prioritize diversity and inclusion are not only more just and equitable, but they also perform better financially. Encouraging diversity and inclusion in any company is a win-win situation for leaders and employees alike.

Research shows that companies with high diversity and inclusion rates are 36 percent more profitable than their less diverse counterparts, which is a huge number and something any leaders concerned about their numbers should take note of. But how we implement effective diversity and inclusion practices is actually more than just a good intention; it requires setting truly actionable strategies in motion. For example, training sessions on diversity and inclusion can help team members recognize and address their biases, which we all have as a product of our backgrounds and upbringing. So, the inclusion of training sessions is a positive first step in implementing these practices.

To take the first step, leaders must first be self-aware of their own biases and then set some guidelines regarding how to create a workplace where these practices are encouraged and in place. Such a change does not take place overnight; rather, the change is cultural and spreads across the whole company. It takes time and patience, so leaders need to provide their teams with the necessary time and support to internalize and bring in those changes. While this may be a gradual approach, it definitely requires a roadmap and a plan to ensure that the new practices are sustainable and impactful.

This is an ongoing journey, not a one-time initiative. It demands continuous effort and regular reflection, and leaders must have a willingness to adapt and grow.

WORKPLACE QUESTIONS

1. First, take a closer look at your current team dynamics and communication practices. How diverse is your team? How open are the channels of communication? Looking at the current state of any organization is always the first step to being self-aware.

_____

_____

_____

_____

_____

2. The next step is to evaluate the company's current state and plan for changes. Rate your company on a scale of 1 to 10 in terms of diversity and inclusivity. What does this score tell you about your company culture? After recording the results, the final step is to implement those changes.

_____

_____

_____

_____

_____

Based on your assessment, implement targeted changes to enhance communication, inclusivity, and diversity, and remember that these changes may require time for your team to adapt. By embracing these principles, leaders can definitely move toward a stronger, more innovative, and more resilient organization, where every team member will feel more valued and empowered to contribute their best.

CHAPTER 7
FOSTERING GROWTH AND RECOGNITION

"What gets recognized gets repeated."
~Michael LeBoeuf

n the journey to building a successful, thriving business or company, professional growth and recognition of each team member are not only beneficial but essential.

This chapter explores how a nurturing environment that encourages personal and professional development and acknowledges achievement can significantly enhance both staff satisfaction and company success.

In my leadership journey, I realized the profound impact of investing in the growth of my team. At the very first startup I worked at, we faced the typical growing pains: rapid expansion, tight budgets, and the constant pressure to innovate, adapt, and change based on our customers' requirements. Despite these challenges, I saw how the company made conscious decisions to allocate resources for staff training and development. That was at the very beginning of my career, and I remember thinking, *How are they able to afford this training and development budget?* But what I saw in the long run, even after I left that company, was success in leaps and bounds.

Staff training and development is an amazing investment that not only enhanced their capabilities but also created a culture of loyalty and commitment that really pushed the company forward. It does seem like a very obvious investment into the training and growth of the people of the company, but all companies and organizations invest at different levels and in different ways. But this is a great area if the leaders of the company are intentional and can make a real difference in all team members' lives, their futures, and the company's future. While this is obvious to us, it is also backed by researchers' statistics that, together, form a compelling narrative. According to a LinkedIn report,[1] 94 percent of employees are likely to stay longer at a company that invests in their career development.

---

1. LinkedIn Learning, *2018 Workplace Learning Report*, accessed 2024, https://learning.linkedin.com/resources/workplace-learning-report-2018?src=li-scin&veh=7010d000001BicLAASv2&cid=7010d000001BicLAAS&bf=1.

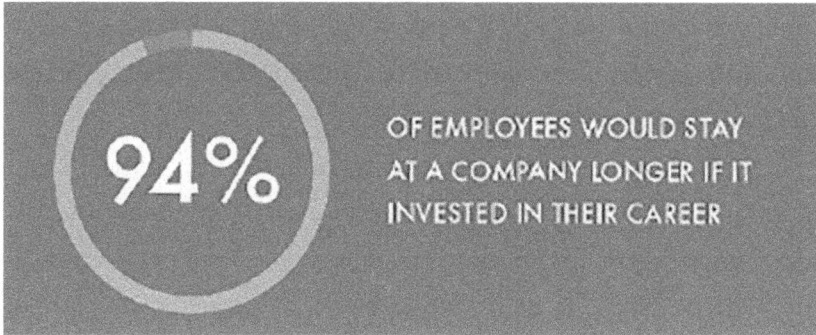

Figure 8. Employee retention LinkedIn.

If the company invests in the career development of its employees, they will stay in their roles for longer, which thus strengthens the company's security and unity. I would also like to emphasize that the cost of employee turnover is huge, ranging from 100 to 200 percent of merely investing in the same employees. Turnover is detrimental to the success of any company and something to always bear in mind. Training and building your own staff, which is in place right now, is way more beneficial than just having them leave and keep hiring new staff. And 75 percent of employees agree that job-related training and opportunities influence their decision to stay with an employer. Hence, there is a clear connection between professional growth and employee retention.

Training and development tell us the importance of continual investment in learning and development programs. And like we said earlier, it has a direct link to profitability and does more than reduce turnover; it directly enhances your company's performance because well-trained employees perform better, leading to high-quality work and improved customer service. When employees feel better, they feel confident, and you're also adding skills to their profile. If your staff work in customer service, for example, their satisfaction and confidence show. As they become more competent and confident, they take greater ownership. We talked about ownership in the previous chapter.

As the employees take ownership of their roles, trust is built, thus deepening their commitment to the company's mission. A win-win situation involves several implementation methods, and every company develops its own. For example, the company I ran had some mandatory training that the company provided. However, there is much more to training and development, with numerous strategies available to implement. More than creating a culture that promotes growth, implementing successful training and development programs requires more than just offering training; it requires a strategic approach tailored to the needs of each individual.

INTENTIONAL TRAINING

Among the various approaches, number one on the list is intentional training—starting with where a team member is. Intentional training starts with a one-on-one performance review, which allows us to assess the specific needs of each team member based on their performance and KPIs.

This targeted approach ensures that the training is not only relevant but also empowering. This is a good starting point. You're providing training that the staff member benefits from and can truly resonate with.

OPEN COMMUNICATION

The second approach is open communication as a leader. Regularly engage with team members to understand their challenges and aspirations, what they really want, and where they want to be one year and five years from now. Also, enquire about any current difficulties, challenges, or knowledge base they're struggling with. Listen with intent and then engage in dialogue rather than deliver a monologue. Above all, ask your employees what they need from you.

PROMOTE FROM WITHIN

The third approach for growth is promoting from within, which should not be overlooked. When hiring a director position, look around your team before considering anyone external to your company. Is there someone, a senior team member, who can take on that position with some additional training?

If you're promoting from within, how much will the hire save the company? Also, it should be noted that hiring from within builds up team morale, as employees can become aware of their own growth opportunities and aspire to ascend in the company. This is a great strategy to employ. Implementing mentorship programs that pair senior team members with newer employees will facilitate skill transfer while also identifying potential leaders or those to promote from within.

SUPPORT EXTERNAL EDUCATION

Another great way to recognize those team members and motivate employees is by plotting clear trajectories for advancements. This is the fourth approach: supporting external education. If a company or leadership encourages and supports team members in pursuing degrees or certifications outside of the company providing training, this is a great benefit to offer. If you're doing a tuition reimbursement or a part of the tuition, you really demonstrate your commitment to ensuring the long-term growth and success of the staff. So, those are some things that can be employed to foster growth.

I would like to talk about mentorship some more because it's an effective way to build a team. The strength of mentorship programs lies in creating more growth and preparing staff for upward mobility through imparting valuable knowledge and insight. In turn, newer employees gain personalized guidance on how to move through the company and how to conduct their tasks more efficiently. This close mentor-mentee relationship enables leaders to closely observe and nurture the unique strengths of each team member, allowing them to easily identify and then prepare employees for future leadership roles.

Recognition goes hand in hand with growth. Regularly acknowledging the achievements and efforts of your team boosts morale and drives confidence and performance. It should be both formal, like an award or a public acknowledgment during meetings, a note of appreciation, or spontaneous commendation for good work. Recognition can bring out your employees' potential and should be demonstrated regularly.

I have seen firsthand how a team member's eyes light up when we show appreciation for something that they did or achieved. Recognition is a simple way of helping teams or team members grow, feel encouraged, and learn new things. Therefore, building a culture that prioritizes growth and recognition is not merely a strategy for reducing turnover, but a way to boost long-term motivation. This chapter concludes with a few more open-ended questions and action steps.

WORKPLACE QUESTIONS

1. The first questions relate to reviewing current opportunities. What do we have in place right now? What kind of strategies do we have? What learning and growth opportunities are we offering? Are they meeting the needs of your team members? Take a hard look at where the company is.

_____
_____
_____
_____
_____

2. After doing some self-reflection, the second area to focus on is planning for new initiatives. If there are any new initiatives that your company needs to put in place, identify which new training programs or growth initiatives can be introduced. Consider areas like leadership training, technical skills, soft skills development, or any job-specific training. Open up communication with the team and assess where they are struggling.

_____
_____
_____
_____
_____

3. The third area is recognition practices, which is about developing a systematic approach to recognizing and rewarding employees. For example, setting regular, let's call them formal recognition times, every two weeks or every month to hold an employee of the month award. A formal reward system, or simply being intentional about informally appreciating employees' efforts, is a good gesture to make. What can you do to make this a regular practice? Through intentional development and genuine recognition, you can truly transform your workplace into a dynamic environment.

_____

_____

_____

_____

_____

It is important to remember that a good company environment is where every team member not only sees a future for themselves but also feels that the company allows them to grow over the years, even when they're not at the company. Successful implementation of staff appreciation results in company success and employee motivation to perform at their best.

CHAPTER 8
CREATING A POSITIVE WORKPLACE ATMOSPHERE

"Pleasure in the job puts perfection in the work."
~Aristotle

I see that the heartbeat of every successful organization is culture. This is a very true statement. A positive workplace atmosphere not only elevates employee happiness but also boosts productivity and creates a spirit of collaboration. In a positive workplace, everyone wants to come in every day, feels good about it, and feels great to be a part of it. When I look back at all my different workplaces, I remember in an instant how I felt there.

And that is what culture is all about. How does the overall picture make you feel? Among the plethora of research on the subject, I want to explore some data-driven insights into how leaders can create an environment that thrives on enthusiasm, engagement, and happiness. As stated in an earlier chapter, happy bees make tasty honey. As such, the general feeling among staff directly correlates with company performance. It is also shown through the quality of your product and customer service to the customer.

In my early years as a team leader in the startup I was at, I saw firsthand the transformative power of a positive work environment. Our team faced intense deadlines and high stakes, but it was the positive atmosphere we cultivated that often saw us through.

I remember the staff saying how exhausted they were at the end of the day, but they were happy. They wanted to come back to work every day for that feeling of satisfaction. Studies show that happy employees are approximately 12 percent more productive, while those who are unhappy are 10 percent less productive.

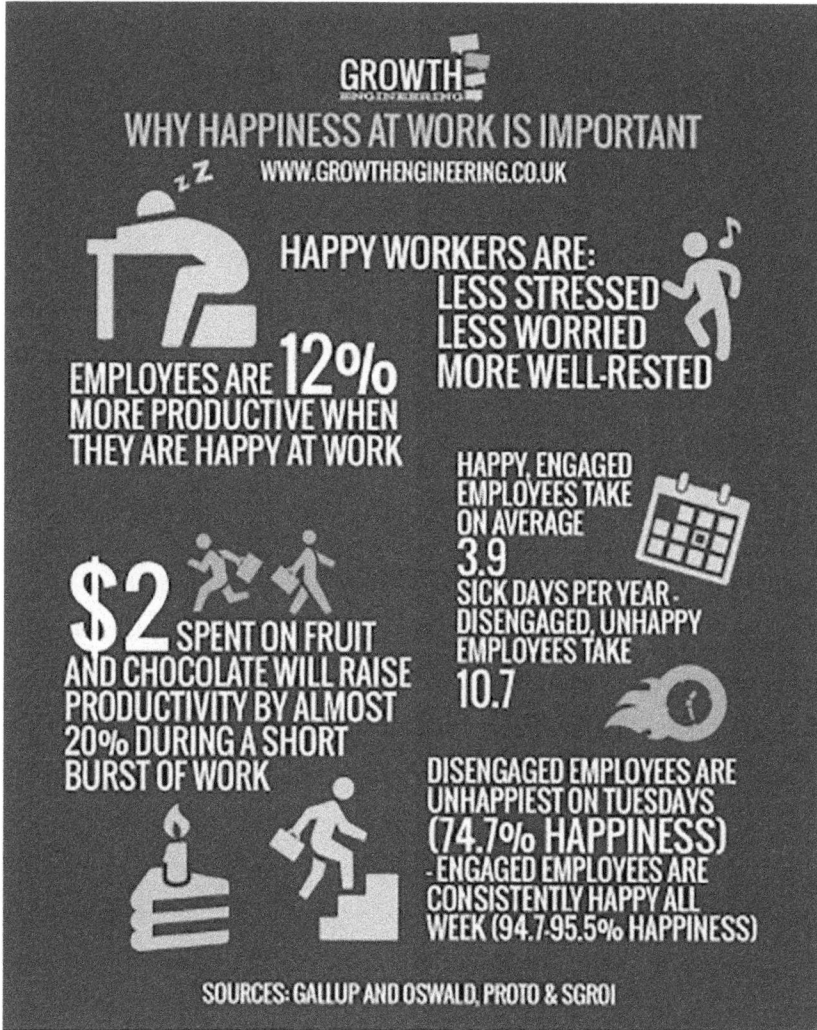

Figure 8. Why happiness at work is important.
(Source: Gallup et al.)[1]

---

1. Most Loved Workplace, "Happy Employees Make the World Go Round: Why Employee Happiness Is Important in 2023," accessed November 22, 2024, https://mostlovedworkplace.com/happy-employees-make-the-world-go-round-why-employee-happiness-is-important-in-2023/.

Furthermore, companies that promote a communal culture, a happy culture, are five times more likely to be high-performing. It is known that happy employees will work better, but research and data really put a stamp on it.

A positive workplace culture is more than just good vibes; it's a strategy, a strategic asset. Remembering personal milestones like birthdays and work anniversaries and organizing team-building events play a critical role in developing this culture. The strategy must be intentional and planned out. There need to be favorites lists, as I recall from my tenure, which we placed in binders to be passed around the staff members.

Those binders included every upcoming birthday or work anniversary, so if someone wanted to buy a gift and send it or give it to the team member, they would be welcome to do so. I have seen leaders and have had at least one boss who would write handwritten notes to their staff members on their work anniversaries, congratulating them and thanking them for their contribution to the company.

In team-building events, the team members often drop their guard and begin to feel comfortable collaborating and learning more about each other. These practices are not just about celebration; they're an acknowledgment of each person's value within the company.

Building long-term workplace loyalty within the teams through care and appreciation reinforces their sense of belonging and appreciation. One of the most impactful team-building activities I initiated was called "Treasure Hunt." This wasn't just a playful escape from daily routines, it was a carefully designed exercise to build trust and friendships among team members. The adventure required collaboration and creative thinking, but most importantly, it allowed team members to interact in new and meaningful ways. There would be one leader, there would be followers, and when everyone felt accomplished, they were able to solve problems and develop collectively. During these moments of shared laughter and challenge, new connections were built, which illustrated how team building can significantly enhance workplace morale and productivity. Imagine doing that, coming to work the next day, and feeling how much lighter the team is feeling, equipped with the ability to work with greater efficiency and productivity.

Here are some practical tips for building a supportive workplace where the support and the positivity of the environment shine. Creating a nurturing work environment involves a series of intentional actions and strategies. Open communication is paramount in an environment where positivity and transparency are encouraged. The value of feedback, innovation, and implementing tools such as the anonymous feedback box encourages team members to bring up their feedback and suggestions anonymously.

I know about a small business owner who was famous and traveled the world. That story always puts a smile on my face. I know that business owner personally, and they are all about having a positive workplace environment. They didn't want to see any gossip or any politics going around because, like a virus, it would be so negative and detrimental to the company's culture. And they were all about building a positive culture where everyone is appreciative of each other.

If they had any feedback, the owner was always available, and we would talk about it. The availability or the accessibility of the leader is essential in these kinds of initiatives in which you are trying to build a positive environment. You need to be open to all feedback and accessible to team members, who can let you know if they see an opportunity for growth anywhere. Remember, there is always room for improvement.

Creating a sense of community is the next point to mention. Encouraging employees to take ownership at every level, where team members feel like they are part of the bigger picture, an integral part of the company, increases their commitment to the company's goals. Employee alignment with the vision and mission of the company fosters a sense of community that we all work toward. Sharing this vision creates a lot of positivity, so supporting a community is an important aspect that any company should focus on. Moreover, staff feel more comfortable and invested in their workplace, and they'll feel more positive about their surroundings, which brings me to the next point: designing and building a positive workspace environment.

Consider the physical environment of the workplace, elements like a coffee station, and indoor plants to add natural life to your workspace. Add a well-equipped break room, like a bookshelf, maybe a reading area. Such amenities will significantly enhance the workplace vibe, making it more inviting, happier, and stimulating. Think about those spas when you enter. They create an inviting atmosphere you can look forward to entering. Such an addition would be ideal in the lobby, break room, or hallway of a workplace.

The next point to cover is promoting continuous improvement. Always seek ways to improve performance through personalized training and growth opportunities. This not only improves skills but also shows a commitment to each team member's personal development.

Overall, staff will feel positive and confident about being a part of the company, which is a reason to celebrate and connect with them. Give out a small cake on a birthday or a shout-out for work anniversaries. These gestures make our team members feel valued, creating even more happiness. We all look forward to such events. I would say the ripple effect of a positive environment and culture is that it enhances all aspects of the office. When the employee or team member feels good, it will positively impact business performance. In a clutter-free environment, employees who feel valued and happy are more creative, more committed to their organizations' vision, and more proactive in their roles.

This will definitely lead to better individual performance and also elevate companies' overall success. I don't want to forget about leadership because everything comes down to leadership. Leaders need to have courage and embrace a vision.

- How do you visualize your company's workplace in terms of appearance and atmosphere?
- Does that vision include the happiness and well-being of your team?
- And does that vision require courage, thinking outside the conventional corporate box, and daring to put people before numbers?

Have no fear; the numbers will come. Don't worry about it. This is the best investment that can be made to ensure a positive workplace environment. And by honoring this vision, you're not just building a business, you're nurturing a culture that can change the world.

WORKPLACE QUESTIONS

1. Assess your current situation. How happy are your employees on a scale of one to ten? To gather this data, you can conduct surveys or have formal or informal discussions. You can even construct an anonymous survey, then do the self-awareness, self-reflection part, and finally, identify areas of improvement based on the feedback.

_____

_____

_____

_____

_____

2. Next, identify where your workplace atmosphere could improve. Is it communication in the workplace, is it through personal recognition, or perhaps the physical environment itself?

_____

_____

_____

_____

_____

Knowing the answers to the above questions will identify precisely where to implement changes. Choose wisely, and take each step as it comes.

Some of the things you can set in motion, and others you can't. Whatever the project, start by taking baby steps. Being intentional

BEYOND THE BOTTOM LINE

should always be the first step, and then you can continue with one or two specific actions to immediately enhance the workplace atmosphere. This could be anything from introducing a monthly team outing to redesigning the office layout or just bringing in a few indoor plants to make the workplace more visually appealing and with a fresher feel.

By taking these steps, you will see an improvement in the energy generated around the workplace and truly begin to transform your workplace into a vibrant and productive workplace where all the team members feel comfortable and motivated to contribute their best.

CONCLUSION

We've reached the end of our shared journey, our exploration of the beautiful and challenging world of organizational culture. Through the highs and lows, the complexities and the simplicities of creating and cultivating the invisible force that drives every organization. Over the course of this book, we covered the undeniable link between positive culture and revenue and how the power of culture can change or transform the fortune of a business. We also looked at the importance of communication, the essence of employee engagement, and the need for a shared vision. Overall, many elements contribute toward fostering a shared vision; among them, a major emphasis should be placed on leadership. As I've touched upon in almost every chapter, leaders need to be intentional about building a great culture in their company. This is what led them to build a great culture in their company. I also delved into the common challenges and hurdles and some ways to overcome them.

The lessons, examples, insights, and strategies we have explored are all stepping stones toward building cultures that are both impactful and profitable. Through this book, we have discovered that the secret the most successful organizations hold is their culture, which, when built correctly and with intention, can be the greatest asset to any company or any business. It is without doubt the heartbeat of any organization, the positive force that propels it forward, and the glue that binds everyone together. Equipped with this knowledge and the tools that you have gained from this book, I trust that I provided you with some light bulb moments, experienced a shift in perspective, and gained new knowledge. You have the power to shape a culture that not only boosts profits but also creates an environment where everyone thrives and is happy. To wrap things up, I want to leave you with a few final thoughts. Remember, creating a positive culture isn't a one-time thing or one-time task or event; it's a continuous journey, a group habit. You must have heard that a habit takes at least 21 days of repetitive action to develop and a year of consistency. When we apply this to an entire company, small or big, it requires commitment, consistency, and, most of all, courage.

Developing a good culture starts with courageous and intentional leadership. You must know that every effort you make, every step you take toward shaping your culture, is never wasted and is a step toward a more impactful, more profitable, and more fulfilling future for your organization. Thank you for taking this trip with me. I'm grateful for your time, engagement, and intention to dive deep into the world of company culture.

I hope that this book provided you with valuable insight, practical strategies, and the inspiration to take action. As our journey comes to a close, another one begins. The knowledge and insight gained from this book are the seeds. It's up to you to plant them, nurture them, and watch them grow. The possibilities are endless, and I can't wait to see you thrive and win. And before we get on with life, I want to extend an invitation to stay connected.

I would love to hear about your experiences, what you took away from this, and how you implemented your successes and challenges as you navigate the world of culture. Feel free to reach out to me, engage with me on social media, and visit my website for more resources. You can reach me on LinkedIn and through my website at the following links: [LinkedIn - https://www.linkedin.com/in/gigiguptadfw/ Website - https://peakblaze.com/].

Finally, to further support your journey, I would like to introduce you to my comprehensive organizational culture transformation program designed to help leaders like you create and sustain a positive, profitable, and impactful culture. I encourage you to check out my program to find out how it can complement and enhance the knowledge you gained from this book.

For anyone interested, you are welcome to schedule a meeting with me to discuss whether the training provided through my course would be a good fit for your organization. In conclusion, remember that the culture of your organization is in your hands. With the right strategies, the right mindset, and the right actions, you can shape a culture, drive success, and make a positive impact. I wish you all the best on your journey, and I look forward to hearing about your successes. Here's to creating amazing cultures together!

THANK YOU FOR READING MY BOOK!

Just to say thanks for buying and reading my book, I would like to give you a free bonus gift, a 1-hour consultation & coaching session with me (a $250 value), no strings attached!

Scan the QR Code:

I appreciate your interest in my book and value your feedback as it helps me improve future versions of this book. I would appreciate it if you could leave your invaluable review on Amazon.com with your feedback.

Thank you!